a ﬕﬖ JOR

fROM

OTHER GIFTBOOKS BY HELEN EXLEY:
**A Romp of Naughty Jokes**
**Looking for Mr Right**
**Battle of the Sexes**
**Men! by women**
**The Wicked Little Book of Quotes**
**Ms Murphy's Law**

OTHER BOOKS IN THIS SERIES:
**A Woman's Work is Never Done**
**Too Soon for a Mid-Life Crisis**

Published simultaneously in 2004 by Helen Exley Giftbooks in Great Britain, and Helen Exley Giftbooks LLC in the USA.

12  11  10  9  8  7  6  5  4  3  2  1

Design, selection and arrangement copyright © 2004 Helen Exley
Cartoons copyright © 2004 Rowan Barnes-Murphy
The moral right of the authors has been asserted.

ISBN  1-86187-591-6

A copy of the CIP data is available from the British Library on request.

Printed in China.

**Helen Exley Giftbooks, 16 Chalk Hill, Watford, Herts, WD19 4BG, UK.**
**Helen Exley Giftbooks LLC, 185 Main Street, Spencer, MA 01562, USA.**
**www.helenexleygiftbooks.com**

Acknowledgements: The publishers are grateful for permission to reproduce copyright material. Whilst every effort has been made to trace copyright holders, we would be pleased to hear from any not here acknowledged. COLLEEN DEWHURST: from the New York Times, 17th February, 1974; MAE WEST: Quotations used with permission from The Roger Richman Agency. Judith C. Grant, Margot Thomson published with permission © Helen Exley 2004.

# WHeN I'm good I'm very very good ~ BuT WHeN I'm BAD I'm BeTTeR!

MAE WEST

Rowan Barnes-Murphy

A HELEN EXLEY GIFTBOOK

"UNTIL YOU'VE LOST
YOUR REPUTATION,
YOU NEVER REALLY REALIZ
WHAT A BURDEN IT WAS."

MARGARET MITCHELL (1900~1949)

A girl can wait
for the right man to come along,
but in the meantime
that still doesn't mean
she can't have fun
with all the wrong ones.

CHER, B.1946

If you obey all the rules
you miss all the fun.

KATHARINE HEPBURN (1907-2003)

"IF I HAD MY LIFE
TO LIVE AGAIN,
I'D MAKE
THE SAME MISTAKES,
ONLY SOONER."

TALLULAH BANKHEAD (1903~1968)

"Goodness, what beautiful
diamonds."
"Goodness had nothing to do with it,
dearie."

MAE WEST (1893-1980),
FROM THE FILM "NIGHT AFTER NIGHT"

I am pure as the driven slush.

TALLULAH BANKHEAD (1903-1968)

> "WHAT RIDICULOUS THING
> WILL YOUR GUY
> DO FOR SEX?
> ANYTHING. HE'S A MAN."
>
> MARGOT THOMSON, B. 1943

A student undergoing
a word-association test was asked
why a snowstorm put him in mind of sex.
He replied frankly:
"Because everything does."

HONOR TRACY

Breathes there a man with soul so dead
Who never to his wife hath said:
Breakfast be damned, come to bed.

SAMUEL HOFFENSTEIN

"TOO MUCH
OF a GOOD THING
CAN BE
WONDERFUL."

MAE WEST (1893~1980)

There are things
that happen in the dark
between two people
that make everything that happens
in the light seem all right.

ERICA JONG, B.1942

SEX?
The most fun I ever had without laughing.

WOODY ALLEN

"Thanks that was great!
That's the best sex
I've ever had with him.
Next time let's get
him to do that
wiggling thing again!"

JUDITH C. GRANT, B. 1960

SO THAT THEY'LL
have SOMEONE
TO TALK TO
when he falls asleep."

ALLAN AND BARBARA PEASE

"MEN aRE
THOSE CREATURES
WITH TWO LEGS
AND EIGHT HAND."

JAYNE MANSFIELD   (1932~1967)

After a man finds out
that the woman is no angel,
he tries to ascertain
to what extent she isn't.

AUTHOR UNKNOWN

No man ever stuck his hand up your dress
looking for a library card.

JOAN RIVERS, B.1933

Only one man
in a thousand is a leader of men —
the other 999 follow women.

GROUCHO MARX (1890-1977)

A man is two people,
himself and his cock. A man always
takes his friend to a party.
Of the two, the friend is nicer,
being more able to show his feelings.

BERYL BAINBRIDGE, B.1934

"I LIKE TO
WAKE UP
FEELING
A NEW MAN."

JEAN HARLOW (1911~1937)

I love men like some people
like good food or wine.

GERMAINE GREER, B.1939

"A WOMAN
CAN LOOK BOTH
MORAL AND EXCITING~
IF SHE ALSO LOOKS
AS IF IT WAS QUITE
A STRUGGLE."

EDNA FERBA (1887~1968)

Sex appeal is fifty per cent
what you've got,
and fifty per cent what people
think you've got.

SOPHIA LOREN, B.1934

What a man enjoys
about a woman's clothes
are his fantasies of how she would
look without them.

BRENDON FRANCIS (ATTRIBUTED)

Happiness is seeing your
favourite girl in a two-piece outfit
– slippers.

BURT REYNOLDS

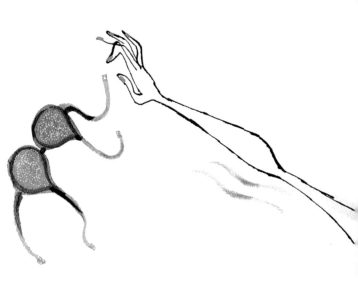

"You can seduce a man
without taking
anything off, without
even touching him."

Rae Dawn Chong

God gave women
intuition and femininity.
Used properly,
that combination easily
jumbles the brain
of any man I've ever met.

FARRAH FAWCETT, B.1948

"MY COMPUTER~DATING
BUREAU CAME UP WITH
A PERFECT GENTLEMAN.
STILL, I'VE GOT ANOTHER
THREE GOES."

SALLY POPLIN

Playful female mouse
seeks shameless male louse.

CLASSIFIED AD

We modern women aren't as prim
as our grannies used to be.
We still have our virtue,
but we hardly ever use it any more.

CATHY HOPKINS

"The girl speaks
eighteen languages
and can't say no
in any of them."

Dorothy Parker (1893~1967)

"Every man
wants a woman to appeal
to his better side
and his nobler instincts~
and another woman
to help him forget them."

Helen Rowland (1875~1950)

"A pessimist
is a man
who thinks
all women are bad.
An optimist is one
who hopes they are."

CHAUNCY DEPEW (1834~1928)

# When women go wrong, men go right after them.

MAE WEST (1893-1980),
FROM THE FILM
"SHE DONE HIM WRONG"

"The best way
to get the better
of temptation is just
to yield to it."

Clementina Graham

"A little she strove,
and much repented,
and whispering,
I will ne'er consent
~ consented."

George, Lord Byron (1788~1824)

CHRISTINA: I love men!
Their company, their talk...
the smell of man's sweat
in the saddle!
I love them in the bone...
in the flesh... the wildness...
the prickly insolence.

PAM GEMS, B.1925

I dig skin, lips and Latin men.

MADONNA, B.1958

There's something about a man
with a whacking great erection
that [is] hard to resist.

DORIS LESSING, B.1919

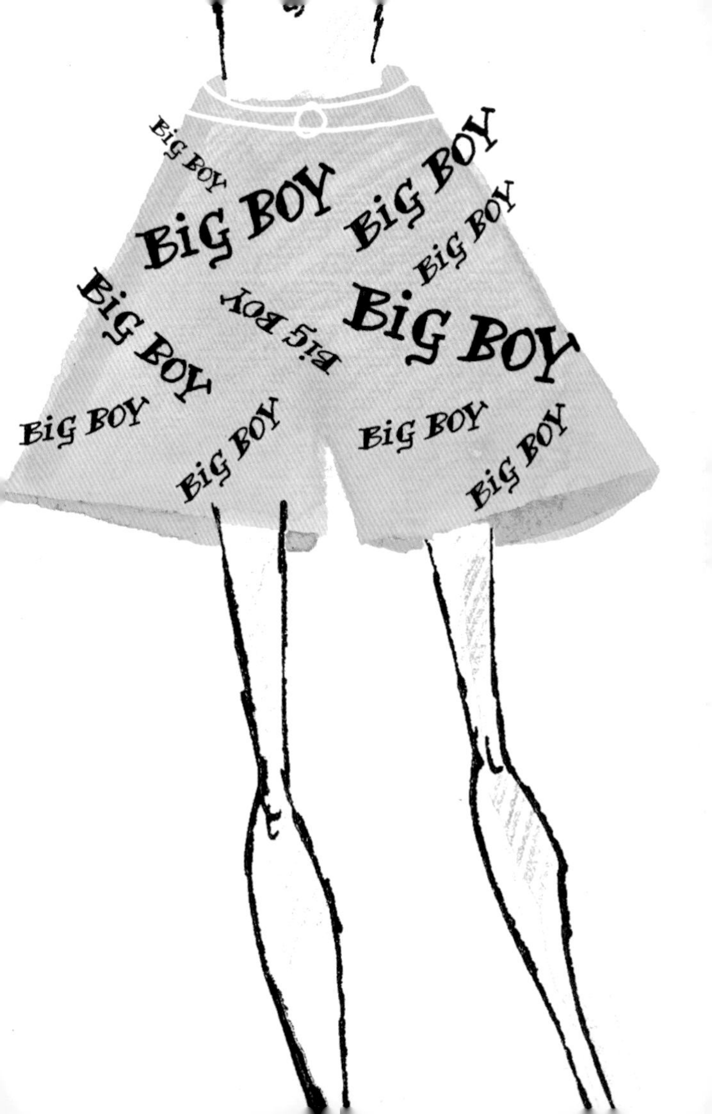

# GENTLEMEN PREFER BLONDES

That gentlemen prefer blondes
is due to the fact that,
apparently, pale hair, delicate skin
and an infantile expression
represent the very apex of frailty
which every man longs to violate.

ALEXANDER KING

As for blondes having more fun,
well, let me dispel that rumour forever.
They do.

MAUREEN LIPMAN, B.1946

WHEN I first MET
ROBERT, who IS 18
years younger
THAN ME, I said
"HE'S BEAUTIFUL.
I LiKe him.
HAVE him STRIPPED,
WASHED AND
BROUGHT TO MY
TENT!"

CheR. B.1946

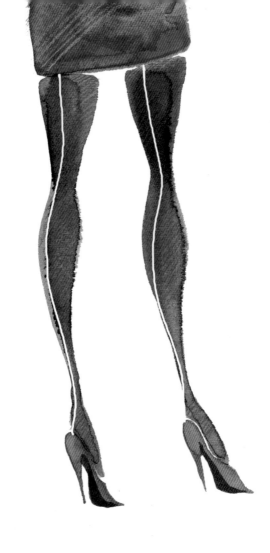

"Seamed stockings
aren't subtle but
they certainly do the job...
If you really want
your guy paralytic
with lust,
stop frequently
to adjust the seams."

CYNTHIA HEIMEL, B.1947

My boyfriend says
my dress is so tight he can hardly breathe.

AUTHOR UNKNOWN

A lady is one who never
shows her underwear unintentionally.

LILLIAN DAY

"We're living
in a kind of pallid
emotional time...
When somebody new
approaches you,
you're afraid
you're being approached
according to page 136."

COLLEEN DEWHURST

# "He is every other inch a Gentleman."

Dame Rebecca West (1892~1983)

I think men are very funny.
If I had one of those dangly things
stuffed down the front of my pants,
I'd sit at home all day
laughing at myself.

DAWN FRENCH

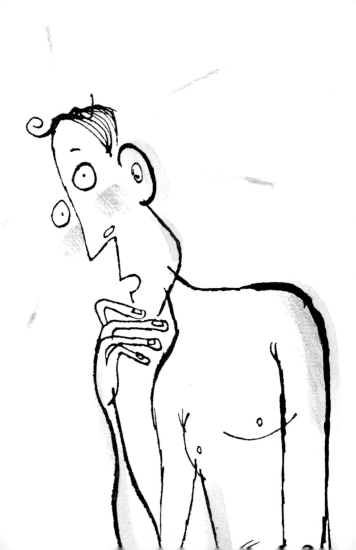

# "Um, Um, Jumbo Please"

...I think if it would help
condom efficiency,
we should package them in different sizes,
and maybe label them
like olives: jumbo, colossal,
and super-colossal,
so that men don't have to go in
and ask for the small.

BARBARA SEAMAN, B.1935

It's been so long since I made love,
I can't remember who gets tied up.

JOAN RIVERS, B.1933

Two old men were sitting in a hotel
and they saw a pretty girl walk past.
"You know," says one to the other,
"you remember that stuff they used to
put in our tea during the War,
to keep our minds off it...?"
"Yes."
"Well, I think mine's beginning to work."

AUTHOR UNKNOWN

An Australian businessman,
who'd had his eye on his secretary
for a long time, was thrilled when she
invited him back to her home on the evening
of his birthday. On their way there
she chatted to him, animatedly,
determined to put him at his ease,
and he felt sure that she was giving him
the come-on. At her flat she gave him
a large whisky and suggested that he take off
his jacket and tie while she popped into
the bedroom for a moment.
Convinced that he was in for a delightful
evening, he took the opportunity
to remove more than his jacket.
In fact he was stark naked when his wife
and his work colleagues emerged
from the bedroom carrying a birthday cake
and everything needed for the party....

AUTHOR UNKNOWN,
FROM "COMIC SPEECHES FOR SOCIAL OCCASIONS"

The only talk I've had on sex
was from an embarrassed headmaster
about the reproduction of lupins.
I'm as ready as can be if ever
I fall in love with a lupin.

MILES KINGTON, B.1941, FROM "MILES AND MILES"

"I hate to tell you
how old I am,
but I reached
the age of consent
75,000
consents ago."

SHELLEY WINTERS, B.1922

The older one grows
the more one likes indecency.

VIRGINIA WOOLF (1882-1941)

There is actually no age limit
to being a slag,
it just gets sadder as you get older.

JENNY ECLAIR

"NO WOMAN
IS EVER OLD ENOUGH
TO KNOW BETTER."

KATHY LETTE. B. 1958

The best lover of all is
the upper-middle-class intellectual.
Having been made to run round
by his mother when he was young
he's into role reversal
and a woman having
as much pleasure as a man.
Lucky the girl that lays
the golden egghead.

JILLY COOPER, B.1937

Do I lift weights?
Sure. Every time I stand up.

There's that old saying
"If God had meant for us to fly,
he'd have given us wings."
Well, look at what he did give us.

DOLLY PARTON, B.1926

"MY BRAIN?
IT'S MY SECOND
FAVORITE
ORGAN."

WOODY ALLEN

**Q**: What's that useless piece of
flesh at the end of a willy called?
**A**: A Man.

GRAFFITO

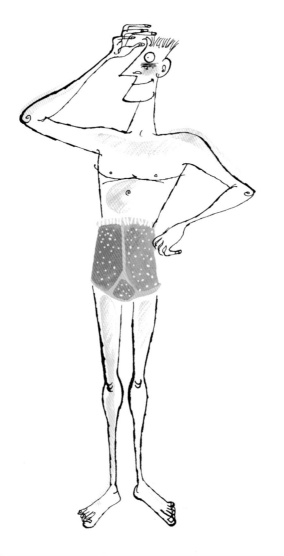

# To err is human – but it feels divine.

MAE WEST (1893-1980)

The follies which a person regrets
the most in life,
are those which we didn't commit
when we had an opportunity.

HELEN ROWLAND (1875-1950)

"AT SEVENTY
YOU STILL GET THE URGE
BUT CAN'T REMEMBER
WHAT FOR EXACTLY."

AUTHOR UNKNOWN

...a raid on a South Carolina brothel
resulted in the arrest of 800 men.
In the days that followed the Sheriff
responsible for the case received dozens
of calls from men asking
that he remove their name from the list —
and one from an elderly man
who offered him $100 to have his name added.

AUTHOR UNKNOWN,
FROM "COMIC SPEECHES FOR SOCIAL OCCASIONS"

The phone went in the house
and I answered it
and this voice said, "Hello,
how would you like a dirty weekend
in Paris?"
And then there was a silence
and the voice said,
"I'm sorry. Have I shocked you?"
And I said,
"God no – I was just packing."

HELEN LEDERER

It used to be boy meets girl,
boy falls in love with girl,
boy marries girl.
Now it's boy meets girl,
boy goes to bed with girl,
boy and girl analyse one another's feelings,
boy decides he's not ready
for a commitment
and girl says she needs her space...
and boy and girl split.
But not before one last bonk.

SHARON DWYER

Rio de Janeiro police
were ordered on a crusade
against women
on the city's beaches
clad in bikinis which,
officials said,
were too revealing.
"We face a difficult
but wonderful challenge,"
said a police spokesman.

WALTER KANITZ, FROM "THE SPEAKER'S BOOK"

# Men aren't attracted to me by my mind. They're attracted to me by what I don't mind.

GYPSY ROSE LEE (1914-1970)

# HELEN EXLEY

Helen Exley has been collecting
and editing material for her
books for twenty-seven years and
still enjoys complete involvement
with each new title.

Her individually conceived and
selected books have now sold
fifty-six million copies since
Exley Publications was formed in
1976. They are now found in
thirty-nine languages on
bookstalls as far apart as Delhi
and Durban, Bridgetown and
Santa Barbara.

# Rowan Barnes-Murphy

Rowan Barnes-Murphy's cartoons are
wicked, spiky and frayed at the edges.

His fantastically well-observed
characters are hugely popular
and have been used to advertise a
diverse range of products such
as cars, clothes and phones,
supermarkets, bank accounts
and greeting cards.

For more information contact:
**Helen Exley Giftbooks, 16 Chalk Hill,**
**Watford, Herts. WD19 4BG, UK.**
**Helen Exley Giftbooks LLC,**
**185 Main Street, Spencer, MA 01562, USA.**
www.helenexleygiftbooks.com